THE TALE OF THE
MIRACLES OF GERASIM OF VOLOGDA

Translated by: Tatiana Ivanovich, D.P. Curtin

THE TALE OF THE MIRACLES OF GERASIM OF VOLOGDA

Copyright @ 2023 Dalcassian Press

All rights reserved. No part of this publication may be reproduced, distributed, or transmitted in any form or by any means, including photocopying, recording, or other electronic or mechanical methods, without the prior written permission of the publisher, except in the case of brief quotations embodied in critical reviews and certain other non-commercial uses permitted by copyright law. For permission request, write to Dalcassian Press at dalcassianpublishing at gmail.com

ISBN: 979-8-8693-7834-7 (Paperback)

Library of Congress Control Number:
Author: Curtin, D.P. (1985-)

Printed by Ingram Content Group, 1 Ingram Blvd, La Vergne, Tennessee

First printing edition 2023.

THE TALE OF THE MIRACLES OF GERASIM OF VOLOGDA

THE TALE OF THE MIRACLES OF GERSIM OF VOLOGDA

Miracles and deeds and the glorious new creation of our venerable and ever-memorable father Gerasim, who planted at the top of the Most Holy Trinity, from the field from Priluk, which is near the Kaysar stream.

Even at this time, God performs glorious and wondrous miracles with His saints everywhere, as God wills, the Lord says: For the one who glorifies me, I will glorify.

Knowledge about the Venerable Father Gerasim, the Vologda miracle worker, and about his miracles. This reverend father of ours Gerasim, the Vologda miracle worker, is hidden in the middle of the world and does not hide in any way, but on faith he places his miracles, and he exudes healing richly from God's spirit to those who come to him with faith. People, having seen and not understanding, did not even think of such a thing, like grace and mercy on his saints and visitation among the elect.

MIRACLE I
Goodness is God's love for mankind and the miracles of his saints who pleased him should always be remembered. What happened in the last times in many selected holy miracles is this new and glorious miracle, which we saw with our eyes under Archbishop Markell of Vologda and Great Perm. Below, let us keep silent about the miracles of the saint for the common benefit and example of those who want to live virtuously, so that we do not sink into the depths of oblivion. From now on, having called the Son of God, I begin the story of the miracles of the venerable Father Gerasim.
There was a certain man, the son of Jacob Saveliev, in the Vologda district, Olarevskaya volost, the village of Bardikha because of Maega, grieving with his feet for a long time, thirty weeks or more, and could not walk in any way, and called many doctors to him, and not a single one You can get a lot of help yourself. And for this reason, the venerable Father Gerasim, the Vologda wonderworker, appeared to him and said to him: Jacob, Jacob, command your children to come to me in the chapel, in the Trinity Monastery, and serve a

THE TALE OF THE MIRACLES OF GERASIM OF VOLOGDA

requiem mass at my tomb, and by the grace of God you will be healthy from this sorrow. And from that appearance he, Jacob, had relief from his grief for ten days or more. He did not do the commandment of the monk, for the sake of oblivion. And when he delayed, Jacob sent him the first bitter sorrow, and lay with that sorrow for about nine days, and again the venerable father Gerasim appeared to him and spoke to him in the same way as the first. At that very hour Jacob ordered himself to lead his children to the monk to pray. And having arrived at the Trinity Monastery, he ordered the reverend Father Gerasim to sing that requiem service to the priest in the chapel. And at the funeral service of the requiem, he kindly kissed the tombstone icon of the saint, and put holy water into his mouth, and took the earth from his shrine, and rubbed his sore feet. And by the mercy of God and the prayers of the Monk Gerasim, at that hour he became healthy from that sorrow at the holy tomb relentlessly. And all that existed glorified God, and Jacob promised to write an image in the name of the saint and to come to his tomb for all the years in memory of him.

This is not the first miracle of our holy and reverend father Gerasim, but many and varied before this healing and appearance, and forgiveness from him, but in oblivion, not given over to the scriptures. For this reason, this miracle of the saint was ordained to happen, having already been witnessed by the great lord, Eminence Markell, Archbishop of Vologda and Great Perm, in the one hundred and fifty-seventh year, on the sixth day of July, when Jacob received mercy from the saint relentlessly at his tomb. And that Jacob's testimony and tale were written before Archbishop Markell by his official clerk Alexey Andreev. And from then on the Most Eminent Marcellus, Archbishop of Vologda and Great Perm, ordered the Trinity priest Gregory to interrogate those who came to the saint, which people had received mercy, and to record ancient and modern miracles in writing, so that they would not pass into oblivion.

And about his residence - how much labor he labored in, and what kind of city he harvested, and what type of rank - we did not find out about this because of many years and from the devastation of the infidels in the city of Vologda. But our rumors extend from the ancient people, who wrote in the old Vologda chroniclers that this venerable father Gerasim's service was all with polyeleos and his Miracles were written for the celebration in memory of the venerable

THE TALE OF THE MIRACLES OF GERASIM OF VOLOGDA

one. And when, by God's instigation, sin for our sakes, destruction came to the city of Vologda from the Gentiles, then the Life of the Saint and the Service were lost unknown.

And about the arrival of the venerable one he writes to Sitsa: In the summer of six thousand six hundred and fifty-five, on the ninth day of August, on the tenth day, in memory of the holy martyr Andrei Stratelates, the venerable father Gerasim came from the God-saved city of Kyiv, the same monk of the Glushensky monastery, to Vologda river, even before the conception of the city of Vologda, on the great forest on the Middle Posad of the Resurrection of Christ, the lazy platform of the Malago market, and created a most honorable monastery for the glory of the Most Holy Trinity from the Vologda river at a distance of half a field. And from there the reverend lived thirty-one years and died in the summer of six thousand six hundred and eighty-six, on the fourth day of March, in memory of our venerable father Gerasim, also in the Jordan.

MIRACLE II

In ancient times there were signs and wonders, and glorious appearances from the venerable father Gerasim. There was a certain old wife, after the destruction of the city of Vologda, from the Myronositsa river, blind from the eyes, two for ten years, not seeing anything. Therefore, our reverend father Gerasim appeared to her and said to her: Woman, tell me to lead you to the former Trinity Monastery at the top and sing a requiem service over my tomb, if you do this, you will be healthy. She felt it from a dream and said to him: God's servant Gerasima, how can I, a great sinner, know where you rest, since I am blind; your holy place, a sin for our sakes, was quickly devastated by the invasion of foreigners. Then the saint again spoke to her: If you truly believe, then you will see the glory of God. And the saint asked her for the cloth and said to her: On which grave you find your cloth thrown down in the morning, sing a requiem mass. Early in the morning, that wife ordered to lead him to the saint, and he found his cloth from the northern country in the corner of the monastery and was cast down. And he ordered that a requiem be sung. She herself, having taken up her cloth, washed herself with tears and prayed diligently to him, and abided her eyes with the prayers of the saint. And from there a holy place was told, and many began to come to the holy place to be healed for their ailments. And after a little time, you erected a small chapel over

THE TALE OF THE MIRACLES OF GERASIM OF VOLOGDA

the relics of the saint and built a shrine and wrote an icon in memory in the name of the saint.

MIRACLE III

It is also useful to tell this miracle to the saint. In the summer of the fifty-sixth year, Maya, on the fourth day, the son of the boyar, in the Vologda district, Vozdvizhenskaya volost, village of Shuktova, Spaskago parish, Vasily Maximov, son of Veniamin, came to the Trinity Monastery to the holy father Gerasim, sang a requiem mass, and told the Trinity priest Grigoryo that he was mournful internal corruption for thirty weeks or more, many times led to death. And having heard about this venerable Gerasim, that many healings came from him to those who came to him with faith, he, the aforementioned Vasily, promised to go and pray. And from that hour he would feel relief. And Vasily came to that one to fulfill his vow and prayed with diligence for a long time, and took holy water and milk from his shrine, and departed for his house, glorifying God and the venerable Father Gerasim. Drink it, put it in holy water, and from it you received the mercy of God, and through the prayers of the saint you were healed from that sorrow.

MIRACLE IV

Below this saint we will remain silent about miracles. In the one hundred and fifty-seventh year, on the first tenth day of the month of June, a certain man, named Aniky Ivanov's son, from the Zolotukha River, grieved with his eyes for a long time, about a year and a half or more, and could not walk for the sake of blindness. And he promised to go to Saint Gerasim to pray. His mother Antonida led her son. And having come to the Trinity Monastery, he commanded that priest to sing a prayer service to the Life-Giving Trinity, and to the venerable requiem mass. He himself prayed to the saint with tears and said within himself: Servant of God, reverend Father Gerasima, behold, I am a great sinner, as if you wish, you can heal me from this sorrow; Because you have received grace and power from Christ God for this, to heal all sorrows of man. Have mercy on me, a sinner and unworthy of your servant, forgive me, and let me still see the light of my eyes. Thus may your holy name be glorified. And therefore he kissed the tombstone icon of the saint. And the priest blessed him with the cross and sprinkled holy water on them, and anointed the eyes of the saint from the grave, and little by little he saw clearly in his eyes. And he promised to paint an icon in the name of the saint, and return to his home,

THE TALE OF THE MIRACLES OF GERASIM OF VOLOGDA

giving praise to God and his saint, the Reverend Father Gerasim. And from then on, I was healthy from that sorrow.

MIRACLE V

We have heard a lot from many about this reverend Father Gerasim and about his miracles, but we were only compelled to write this, so that the healing of the saint would not be the end of laziness for the sake of our oblivion. In the year one hundred and fifty, on the fifth day of July, there was a certain man, the son of Arkhip Hierotheus, nicknamed Petukhov, who lived near the saint in Trinity Street. But it happened that he suffered greatly from black infirmity for three years or more, and often from the unclean spirit we are thrown down, and we beat you hard, sometimes in the house, sometimes on the way. And his beating was violent, as if his eyes were closed, and he lay silent, as if dead, for two and three hours. And for this reason, I will remember the reverend Father Gerasim, that many healings came from him. And she came to him in the chapel, prayed diligently to him with warm faith and tears, and ordered a requiem service over the saint's tomb. And pray to the saint himself and pray for him to God. And therefore, I kissed his icon and, having drunk the holy water and taking water and soup, went to my house and drank in the holy water. And from this, through the prayers of the saint, receive the mercy of God and be healthy from that sorrow. And from then on they began to come to the saint all week long, pray to him diligently, and give him praise.

MIRACLE VI

One day the other day, a man named Nahum forged iron from the blacksmiths on the road, grieving with his eyes for twelve weeks. And I didn't see my path at all, and about this poster I prayed to God, so that I would receive my sight even a little. One night Father Gerasim appeared to him and commanded him to sing a requiem mass on his tomb. In the morning, he stood up and commanded to be led to the saint, and sang the funeral service, and kissed the saint's tombstone icon, and the priest sprinkled it with holy water, and took the chest from the saint's tomb, and rubbed his eyes, and received health from that sorrow. And from then on, she began to maintain great faith in the saint and to bring two pennies from her labors every week, and until her end.

MIRACLE VII

THE TALE OF THE MIRACLES OF GERASIM OF VOLOGDA

The times before this, in the one hundred and fifty-ninth year, on the thirtieth day of November, there was a certain man named Leonty Elizason, of the Vologda district, Syamzhenskaya volost, Spaskago parish, a peasant, mourning with his feet for a year and a half and more. And you can't walk as fast as you can and call for a lot of doctors. And because of this, the doctor gave away not a little of his property, and he did not receive help from the doctors, but the first thing he suffered was bitter. And you fall into a great and great relaxation. After some time, having heard about this venerable Gerasim and about his miracles, he immediately ordered to be led to the saint. And bringing him into the chapel, he ordered a requiem to be sung. He himself fell before the image of the saint and prayed to him diligently, and from his eyes like two sources of tears flowed. And after prayer, he stood up and kissed the image. And from that hour you received mercy from God through the prayer of the venerable one, and you were healed of that disease.

MIRACLE VIII
Some days later in the same year, on the third day of December, there was a certain man named Simeon Bogdanov, the son of Vologda district, from Shirogorye, the village of Onanina, who had a daughter named Akolina. She received a visit from God, having grieved with her eyes for about three years. Therefore, her father went to St. Gerasim and ordered the requiem service to be sung in the chapel, and the priest sprinkled holy water on her eyes, and rubbed the saint's face. And suddenly, through the prayers of the saint, he received from God the gift of forgiveness from that illness, glorifying and thanking the Holy Trinity and the Venerable Father Gerasim.

MIRACLE IX
At the same time, the same year, Maya, on the seventh day on the tenth day, a certain wife named Glykeria Ivanova, daughter of Feofilaktov, wife of Skornyakov, with Obukhov, a certain ulcer appeared on her forehead. And that's why she suffered angrily for three days or more, and her whole face and larynx were swollen, and her eyes were numb, and she lay there like she was dead. Her father John, seeing such illness, soon went to the saint. And he came to the Trinity Monastery at evening singing, and stood until dismissal. And according to this he commanded that existing priest to go to the saint in the chapel and sing a requiem. He himself fell before the icon of the saint, asking forgiveness for his daughter, too, rising from prayer and taking the saint's breast

THE TALE OF THE MIRACLES OF GERASIM OF VOLOGDA

from the shrine, and drinking from it to his daughter, smearing her face and throat. And that made her feel better through the saint's prayers. And this wife Glyceria herself came to the saint in the chapel and ordered the requiem to be sung, and a great prayer was given to the saint. And not for many years was she free from her illness through the prayers of the saint.

MIRACLE X

In the year one hundred and sixty, on the eighth day of October, a certain man, named Ignatius Anthony's son, born in Kargopol, lived in a suburb on Lenivaya Square, in the Varvarinsky monastery. I was in the forest cutting wood for work, and he had a visit from God, causing him to have a toothache. And he stopped from his work, and promised to go to Holy Father Gerasim to pray, and from that hour he would feel better. I arrived at my house, and for three days I didn't have a single thought about going to the saint, fulfilling my promise. As he slowed down, the same illness arose again, and his whole face became swollen, and his heart was filled with great melancholy. And he fell on his face, lying silent as if dead. His wife named Varvara, screaming and lifting him up in tears, said: Why, my lord, have you forgotten your vow that you wanted to go to Saint Gerasim to pray. He felt as if he had fallen asleep and felt better from grief. He soon flows to the saint to pray, and again on the way, hating good, the enemy is the devil, and put in his mind the thought that I am working hard, and it is unlikely that we will get help from the saint. His grief began to rise more bitterly than before. He sighed from the depths of his heart and went without a doubt to the saint. And he came to the Trinity Monastery at evening singing, and stood until vacation. And according to this he commanded that existing priest to go to the saint in the chapel and perform a requiem mass. He himself fell before the icon of the saint, asking for forgiveness. And for this reason, he raised and kissed his icon. The priest sprinkled him with holy water and gave him something to drink. And at that time God forgive him from that sorrow through the prayers of the saint at his tomb relentlessly. And I went, rejoicing over the healing, glorifying God and Holy Father Gerasim.

MIRACLE XI

Not many days ago, a certain man came to pray to the saint, named Gabriel Vasilyev, son of the Deacons, from Eremintsev, who had been grieving with fever for a long time. And he came to the saint and ordered a requiem service

THE TALE OF THE MIRACLES OF GERASIM OF VOLOGDA

for the saint. He himself earnestly prayed to the saint, saying: God's servant Gerasima, save me and heal me from sorrow, a great sinner, by the gift of God given to you from above, so that all people who have seen faith will praise your holy name. And he said this, venerating his image. And the priest sprinkled holy water on him. And he took the earth from the holy tomb, and, having reached the house, he drank water from it many times. And through the prayers of the Holy Father, receive illness and health.

MIRACLE XII

In the past, a certain man, named Grigory Afanasyev, son, from the Vologda district, Karachay volost, village of Selishch, mourned with his feet for a long time and called many doctors to him. And there would be no help for him from them. And therefore, having heard about this holy Father Gerasim, that there were many healings from him, and promised to go to him, and he would get relief. He went to the saint and, having come, ordered a requiem service in his chapel, he took the saint's shoes to the ground, and rubbed his feet, and was healthy from that sorrow.

MIRACLE XIII

A certain man, named Gerasim Afanasyev's son, from Old Square, a blacksmith by trade. And there was an ache at the head of his head for about four weeks, and something had sunk into his right ear, and the whole head of his father felt nothing. And remember this holy Father Gerasim and his many miracles and go to him. And he ordered a requiem to be sung at the saint's tomb, and then kissed his icon, and the priest sprinkled holy water on his sore places. And his pinch began at that hour to cease with the prayers of the saint. He took it, and went to his house, rejoicing, and having come to the house, he took some holy water and drank it himself. And by the gift of God and the Holy Father Gerasim, I became healthy.

MIRACLE XIV

The secret of the king is good, it is glorious to preach the works of God, and it is great to glorify his saints. Accordingly, a certain man, named Dometian Alexiev, son of the Vologda district, village of Ryazanka, from the Savior from Brusnishnik, came to pray to the saint. And he told the priest about himself to that priest named Gregory: It happened that I was once in the forest at work and was cutting firewood, and a tree struck me in the shin in the left leg, and it

THE TALE OF THE MIRACLES OF GERASIM OF VOLOGDA

bound my leg, and wild meat began to grow on that wound. And I called many doctors to myself, and there was no help for me from them, and I was completely weakened for twenty weeks, and was unable to move in any way. And having heard from the Reverend Father Gerasim that there were many healings from him, he promised to go to him to pray, and cried to the lord: May he give me at least a little joy. And from that hour things became easier, and the ulcer began to take root on my stomach. And I soon went to the saint, and for this reason I commanded that a requiem mass be sung in the chapel and pray diligently to the saint. And he went to his house, rejoicing and glorifying God and his saint, the venerable father Gerasim, who became healthy from that sorrow.

MIRACLE XV

Just as the sun is covered by dark clouds and its rays of light are like that, so are the miracles of the saints, even if they did not indulge in laziness for the sake of writing, the essence is unsteadily believed, because they think it is wrong, but otherwise. It is not appropriate to hide a lamp under a bushel, but to place it on a candlestick, so that even those who enter can see the light. If we remain silent, the stone will cry out. There was a certain old woman named Sophia who lived at the Resurrection of Christ in Rakulev. Having received a visit from God, she was exhausted in her eyes and could not see anything for thirty weeks or more. And therefore the Reverend Father Gerasim, the Vologda miracle worker, appeared to her and ordered her to behave in the Trinity Monastery, and sing a requiem mass at his tomb, and you will be healthy. Based on this phenomenon, she was in doubt. And therefore, on the third night, the saint appeared to her and spoke the same word to her. She, having woken up from sleep, was afraid of the lords. Soon she ordered to be led to the saint and in his chapel, she ordered a requiem mass. She herself fell before the icon of the saint and prayed, saying: Forgive me, God's servant Gerasima, and pray for me, a great sinner, to the Lord God and the Most Pure Mother of God, and give me still poor light to see. And for this reason, I kissed his image. And the priest sprinkled holy water on her, and she rubbed the holy Persia on her aching eyes. And through the prayers of the Holy Father Gerasim, his aching eyes soon saw clearly. Go to your home, rejoicing and thanking God, for he is generous and merciful, and giving great praise to his saint, for he will soon find those calling for his help.

THE TALE OF THE MIRACLES OF GERASIM OF VOLOGDA

MIRACLE XVI

Just as the smoke drives away the bees, so also our negligence separates us far from God and draws us into eternal fire, just as the Gospel says about the rich Lazarus: See how you humble his sorrow and how chastened his torment. For this reason, lovingly, God punishes us with sorrows and misfortunes, so that through our negligence we do not fall away from God and perish in evil. There was a certain man, named Matthew Martyriev, son of Pyatyshev, who lived near the saint in Trinity Street, cruel and unmerciful. Once he happened to lose his mind, and shouted a lot, and spoke senselessly, and looked at this and ovamo, and raged, madly, against the walls and against the ground. His father Martyrius and mother Euthymia held him tightly in their hands so that he would not harm himself in any way. He, tearing away from them, semo and ovamo, and bit his father on the right hand. They, seeing this, took him to Saint Gerasim in the chapel and laid him on the ground at the saint's tomb. We ourselves began to pray to him diligently, saying: God's servant Gerasima, pray to the Most Holy Trinity for our son and grant him forgiveness and healing from this sorrow, for we will not depart from your holy tomb. And I stood in the chapel all night in prayer before his image with tears. Their son lies as if dead at the holy shrine, speechless. In the morning, their son got up, as if feeling from a heavy sleep, and began to speak meaningfully and pray to God and his holy saint Gerasim. And from that hour the mercy of God was upon him, through the prayers of the Reverend Father Gerasim, he became healthy from that sorrow. And he went to his house, glorifying God, with his parents and the saint of God Gerasim.

MIRACLE XVII

Just as the land is good, and often the seeds sown into it return with a profit, so also miracles for the saints are given to those who come with faith and healings. In the year one hundred and sixty-seven, on the sixth day of July, there was a certain man named Elijah Ananyin, the son of Vologda district, the village of Okatov, a peasant of Joseph Vasilyev, the son of Voronov, who lay on fire for ten weeks or more, and had many dreams and ghosts from demons. , and lying near death. His mother called his spiritual father and ordered him to confess and give him holy communion. After a little time, the sick man fell asleep and heard a voice saying, and not seeing anyone: Elijah, Elijah, do not be afraid of the power of the enemy, but just say the Jesus Prayer and protect yourself with the sign of the cross, and, rising, pray to God, and you will be healthy. He felt

THE TALE OF THE MIRACLES OF GERASIM OF VOLOGDA

better from sleep and felt better from grief. And therefore, I heard about Holy Father Gerasim that many healings came from him. For fear the city does not cover the top of the mountain standing, so this one filmed about its miracles will become more famous. And therefore, I went to the saint in the Trinity Monastery and ordered the singing of a requiem. He himself, praying to the saint, kissed the saint's gravestone icon, and the priest sprinkled it with holy water, and rubbed the saint's Persia. And by God's gift and the prayers of Holy Father Gerasim, he became healthy from that sorrow, and from then made a promise to himself that he would definitely go to the saint every day.

MIRACLE XVIII

Just as a stone magnet attracts iron, or whoever finds beads is honest, so the holy father of life, whom God desires to glorify miracles or the places of their labors for the sake of great deeds, will soon be known. As the imams clearly speak about this holy thing. There was a certain wife, named Theodora Ioannikiev, daughter of Popov, from the Sretensky shore. And after the death of her husband, her mind became weak and she walked as if darkened by darkness, and spoke absurd things for four weeks. Her father, the priest Ioannikios, took his daughter and took her to the holy father Gerasim to pray. And he commanded that living priest to sing a requiem mass at the saint, and then he kissed the saint's tombstone icon, and sprinkled it with holy water, and took the saint's cup, and when he got home, he gave the water from the cup to drink. And soon from the saint you will receive healing from that sorrow through the prayers of the saint. And from then on she made a promise to herself that she would go to the saint for all her years.

MIRACLE XIX

Just as a certain pure source never runs out, just as it abounds in its own rapids, so this saint abundantly pours out healing for various ailments with faith to those who come with faith. In the year one hundred and fifty-seven, on the third day of July, Gryaznoy Ivanov's son came to the Trinity Monastery to pray with his wife and children. He brought his son Kozma for thirty years, mourning with his feet for ten weeks or more. And he carried him into the chapel to the saint. And he commanded a requiem mass and prayer to the saint: let him pray to God for him and give healing to the sick man. And then they kissed the tombstone icon of the saint, and took holy water and earth, and rubbed their sore feet. And little by little his veins began to stretch out with the prayers of the saint, and soon he became healthy from that sorrow.

MIRACLE XX

It's like a chickweed collects small drops of dew from many flowers, and from this she creates food for herself and delights other people, since sweetness is called honey, and light is called day. And the saints are glorified by good deeds and lives and are recognized by miracles, just as this holy father Gerasim boasted, for when he spoke to the righteous, people will rejoice, and the memory of the righteous will be praised, and the blessing of the Lord will be upon his head, and the righteous will be an eternal memory. In the year one hundred and fifty-nine, Maya on the third day, there was a certain man named Martin Tarasiev's son, Bolypago of the clerk's court. It happened that he was overcome by a fever for eleven weeks or more, and it tormented him greatly. For this reason, he remembered the venerable father Gerasim, that he had many healings, and said to himself: Servant of God Gerasim, I know for I am your many-sinful and indecent servant, as if you have found abundant grace from Christ God and a crown of kindness from the hand of the Lord, so and to me, now fierce and suffering from the fire, forgive and have mercy. And he promised to go to the saint to pray, and little by little God ease him from that sorrow with the prayers of the saint. He was joyful and went to the saint. And he came to the Trinity Monastery, and commanded the piebald priest to the existing Life-Giving Trinity a prayer service, and to the venerable Father Gerasim a requiem service. He himself uttered many prayers to the saint and kissed his gravestone icon, and the priest sprinkled him with holy water. And by God's gift and the prayers of Holy Father Gerasim, at that hour he became healthy from that sorrow. And he promised to write and pray in the name of the saint, and to go to the saint throughout the years.

MIRACLE XXI

Who in God began to work the miracles of this holy story. And if anyone desires the honor of their benefit for the sake of the soul, and anything from our spiritual syllables is not corrected in speeches, where something has been rejected or transformed into ignorance or oblivion, and you, my Lords, fathers and brothers, fill your minds with yours, and do not condemn , but remember the apostolic things, about this you bear burdens to each other, and thus fulfill the law of Christ. And again, the Lord says about this: Do not condemn, lest

THE TALE OF THE MIRACLES OF GERASIM OF VOLOGDA

you yourself be condemned, but forgive, lest you yourself be forgiven by God. In this regard, measure in moderation, and it will be measured to you by the righteous judgment of God. Because I, a great sinner, had not been to Athens and had not lived with philosophers, and had not seen any good and sound offensive moral teaching, although I had touched only a little of the Divine Scripture with the teaching. But I, a great sinner, hoped for the help of Almighty God and for him, the saint of the Reverend Father Gerasim. Yes, he will teach me miracles to his writings. With the advice and blessing of the mentor and shepherd of that church, the priest Gregory Alexiev, son of Popov, born in Belozersk, with his nourishment and labors and for many years, he will save me and have mercy on his unworthy servant Thomas, and give the grace of the Holy Spirit, who dared say the word. Accordingly, a certain man came to pray to the holy Father Gerasim, named John, a coppersmith with his wife and children, and ordered a requiem service for the saint. The great man himself was holding a poster and praying at his tomb. And after the requiem service, he told the priest that living thing: Last year my son was unable to do so, he lay like a firebrand for nine weeks or more. And I, a great sinner, came to the holy father Gerasim to pray and took the land from him, and gave his son water to drink with it. And from that, through the prayers of the saint, he would soon be in good health. And from that time on, I, a great sinner, made a promise to myself that throughout the years I would come to the saint and sing litanies at his tomb, and pray diligently, and give great praise for his miracles, for he is so merciful to help.

MIRACLE XXII

Just as it is possible to contain everything in the abyss of the sea into a small particle, so too can we confess the greatness of the works of our great God, who creates saints for those who come with faith everywhere. At the previous time there was a certain wife named Mavra Nesterov, daughter of Panov, from the village of Brsovka. It's been a long time with my feet, about a year and a half or more, and I can no longer walk. And she called many doctors to her, and there was no help for her from them. Therefore, the Monk Gerasim, the Vologda wonderworker, appeared to her and ordered her to sing a requiem mass in his chapel, and from that appearance she would feel better. She forgot and didn't go to the saint for about ten weeks. And again, her illness was more severe than the first, and again the saint appeared to her and said: Why have you forgotten, my wife, my appearance, and why don't you come to me to pray? She, waking

THE TALE OF THE MIRACLES OF GERASIM OF VOLOGDA

up from sleep, soon ordered to be led to the saint and ordered the singing of a requiem. She herself prayed to him diligently and shed many tears at his grave: Have mercy. And they began to stretch out their aching crouched faces and fight against them. And therefore, she kissed his holy image kindly, and took it from the shrine, and rubbed her feet. And at that hour God forgave her through the prayers of the saint at his tomb relentlessly.

She, having given thanks to the Most Holy Trinity for this miracle and to his saint, the Reverend Father Gerasim, went, rejoicing, to her home. They saw that I had come and was healthy, and glorified everything that was holy.

MIRACLE XXIII

If you, beloved fathers and brethren, and for God's sake, I, who am a great sinner before the speech of the holy miracle, commit you to writing, since God has taught you the holy paraclete, the present one is also worthy of being written for the benefit of those who hear, and the saint of those who glorify. About this speech of the Lord: For I will glorify the one who glorifies me, and I will exalt in my boasting. There was a certain wife named Darius Nikiforov, the daughter of Bychinev, a widow, from the Myronositsa shore. She grieved with her left leg from the parable for six weeks or more, the ulcer was on her mold. She had a son named Alexy, and he had great faith in the saint. Tell your mother about this that there are many healings from it. When she heard his word, she soon ordered him to be taken to the saint. And when she arrived, she sang a requiem and took the earth from his coffin, and prayed to him with love and will, and, having arrived home, she rubbed her sore leg with earth. And for a short time she became healthy from that sorrow through the prayers of the saint.

MIRACLE XXIV

After a few days, a certain man came to the saint to pray, the name of Thomas son of Anikiev, nicknamed Luzin, from St. Nicholas the Wonderworker from the Mountain. I was ill due to dental disease for five or more weeks. Yes, at the same time, his son was ill with a celiac disease, and many times his son was dying. And he sang a requiem and then kissed the tombstone icon of the saint, and took some land, and when he got home, he drank the water from it and gave it to his son. And by the grace of God, they became healthy through the prayers of the saint.

THE TALE OF THE MIRACLES OF GERASIM OF VOLOGDA

MIRACLE XXV
Last year, in the year one hundred and fifty-six, on the fifth day of June, a certain man, named Gabriel Victor's son, an icon painter, came to pray to the Holy Father Gerasim. His daughter, a girl of about four years old, was ill with black infirmity for ten weeks or more. When her father promised to pray to the saint and ordered a candle to be found from her, he sang a requiem mass for the saint and set a candle, and took the earth, and when he got home, he gave her water to drink from it, and from that she received health through the prayers of the saint.

MIRACLE XXVI
The venerable father Gerasim from the Myrrh-bearing coast of John Semyonov healed his son and daughter, the girl had been suffering from a celiac disease for four weeks or more.

MIRACLE XXVII
In the year one hundred and fifty, on the fifth day of July, the same Saint Gerasim forgave Gabriel Chadov from Obukhov, and grieved with a fever for about fifteen weeks.

MIRACLE XXVIII
That same year, on the seventh day of October, the Reverend Father Gerasim offered healing from the poor house of Kasma Romanov, his son Kormiltsev, and mourned with his feet for about forty weeks.

MIRACLE XXIX
That same year, on the first day of July, the Reverend Father Gerasim forgave the village of Kukshinov, Grigory Ivanov, who had been grieving with a fever for fifteen weeks.

MIRACLE XXX
In the one hundred and fifty-seventh year, on the fifth day of July, the venerable father Gerasim of the Savior from the village of Vypryagovo healed Danil Ivanov's son Tulkov from the main pain, he grieved with that grief in every month for three or more days for six years.

MIRACLE XXXI

THE TALE OF THE MIRACLES OF GERASIM OF VOLOGDA

In the same year, on the fourth day of August, the Reverend Father Gerasim, the mistress, healed the son of the boyar Alexander Diomidov, the son of Shestakov, who had been grieving with a fever for about eleven weeks.

MIRACLE XXXII
Reverend Father Gerasim healed Faster Serapionov from inside the city, having been grieving with his feet for a year and a half or more.

MIRACLE XXXIII
The Monk Gerasim from Vedensky Street healed Tretyak Methodov, who had been grieving with his teeth for five weeks.

MIRACLE XXXIV
The Monk Gerasim healed Jacob the Baptist from the desert, who had been on fire for seven weeks.

MIRACLE XXXV
The venerable father Gerasim from the Myrrh-bearing shore healed Jacob, a Swedish tailor, who had been ill for about six weeks with fire.

MIRACLE XXXVI
Let us keep silent about the miracles of this saint In the hundred and fourth year, on the twenty-second day of February, the wife of the lifter Vasily Khristoforov, Akilina Evsivieva, came from Kalashnaya streets to the Trinity Monastery to pray to Saint Gerasim. And she said to the Trinity priest Gregory: This year I, a great sinner, grieved with my left foot from the Intercession of the Most Holy Theotokos until the autumn day of St. Nicholas, and for this I will remember the holy Father Gerasim, who works many miracles and healings for those who come to him with warm faith. And I promised to go to him to pray, and that would make me feel better. And after Matins on St. Nicholas's day she came to the saint to pray and sang a requiem, and the priest sprinkled holy water, and took his chest from the shrine, and rubbed her sore leg. And from this God's mercy befall her, the monk forgave her in that hour at his tomb relentlessly. Again, during Great Lent, on the fourth day of March, in memory of the Holy Father Gerasim, she came to pray and told the priest in the chapel in front of everyone how the saint would soon heal her at his tomb relentlessly. And all the people who heard that praised God and his holy saint Gerasim. And

THE TALE OF THE MIRACLES OF GERASIM OF VOLOGDA

for this reason, she prayed to that existing priest, that he would command this miracle to be written down in holy scripture for the benefit of those who hear it, and to lay his hand on her spiritual father, at her request, for the sake of healing, and it was signed.

MIRACLE XXXVII

It is also useful to tell this miracle of the saint and punish those who are careless, and always honor others through the fear of God and his saints. Not many days later, another miracle appeared in the same year, on the seventh day of March, the priest Thomas Andreev's son came to the Trinity Monastery to pray to the saint from the Vologda district, Bryukhovsky volost, Church of the Nativity of Christ, but he told the Trinity priest Gregory that last year he had been unable to use his right eye and had not seen anything for five weeks or more, and had prayed a lot to God, and made vows to the saints, and had not been able to improve his health. And because of this, we heard about this saint that there were many healings from him and promised to go to him to pray. Soon in the evening and in the morning he arose in health, his aching eye received sight. He gave praise to God and his saint, the Reverend Father Gerasim, about this miracle, and ordered his miracles to be written down with the others, and from now on put his hand to it for the benefit of others who heard it, so that the miracles of the saint would not be forgotten. And make a promise to yourself that in the name of the saint, to write an icon and throughout the years to come to him in memory of him to pray and perform requiem services, and to tell others about this saint, how great he is, he is merciful and generous.

THE BREVITY OF THE CHRONICLER

In the summer of six thousand six hundred and fifty-five, on the ninth day of August, on the tenth day, in memory of the holy martyr Andrei Stratelates, the Monk Gerasim came from the God-saved city of Kyiv, who was tonsured in the same weight of the Glushensky monastery, even before the conception of the city of Vologda, to the great forest, to the Middle Posad of the Resurrection of Christ, the Lazy platform of the Small Market, and created from the Vologda River for half a field a temple of honor and a monastery to the glory of the Most Holy and Life-Giving Trinity. From then on he lived for thirty-one years and died in the summer of six thousand six hundred and eighty-six, the month of March on the 4th day, in memory of our venerable father Gerasim, who lived on the Jordan, the beast served him.

THE TALE OF THE MIRACLES OF GERASIM OF VOLOGDA

According to some reliable chroniclers and circumstances, this city can probably be honored among the cities built in the eleventh or tenth century, or even earlier. For in the Life of the Monk Gerasim, the Vologda wonderworker, it is written that he came from Kyiv to Vologda in the year six thousand six hundred and fifty-five, during the reign of Grand Duke Izyaslav Mstislavich, grandson of Vladimir Monomakh, and from the Vologda River half a mile away, on the Kaisarovo stream, and in a mile from the marketplace, which is now called Lazy Square, he built the Trinity Monastery, where there is now a parish church, in the upper part of the suburb, at the end of the city, in which church the tomb of this saint is located.

The Scriptorium Project is the work of a small group of lay people of various apostolic churches who are interested in the preservation, transmission, and translation of the works of the early and medieval church. Our efforts are to make the works of the church fathers accessible to anyone who might have an interest in Christian antiquities and the theological, philosophical, and moral writings that have become the bedrock of Western Civilization.

To-date, our releases have pulled from the Greek, Syriac, Georgian, Latin, Celtic, Ethiopian, and Coptic traditions of Christianity, and have been pulled from sundry local traditions and languages.

THE TALE OF THE MIRACLES OF GERASIM OF VOLOGDA

www.ingramcontent.com/pod-product-compliance
Lightning Source LLC
LaVergne TN
LVHW061044070526
838201LV00073B/5173